Puppy Training

The Complete Guide to Raisii

Gregory Davis

Gregory Davis

CONTENT LISTING:

Puppy Training 101

1

When Your Puppy Comes Home

Welcome to 'Puppy Training 101' - the ideal guide for all puppy owners who need help getting started with training their new little friend. It doesn't matter whether you've had puppies before or this is your first time, it is our hope at DGB Canine Co. that you'll find this guide invaluable as an informative resource.

The goal of this book is to provide you with a detailed yet comprehensive overview of how to properly train your puppy so that they can develop into the best possible adult dogs. 'Puppy Training 101' makes puppy training easy and feasible. A lot of puppy training guides don't take into consideration that not all of us have that much time to train our puppies. That's where this manual comes in. By giving you the tools that you need to raise the perfect dog (in the form of step by step instructions), you can ensure that you will have a healthy and happy puppy on your hands.

What is certain is that dogs, whether you adopt them young or get them old, truly are the best companions that a person could have and they're a veritable blessing. For this reason among so many others, it is completely worth putting in the effort, time and patience needed to raise and train a puppy. This guide will help you to learn and master all the basic steps required for giving your new little family member the perfect home and the best start.

From experience, I certainly know how difficult it is to raise a puppy- especially if you're a first time dog owner. Do not worry though! This book cuts out all the fluff (no pun intended!) and gets right to the important information for raising a puppy. In this guide, every focal aspect of puppy raising and training will be covered. I am also aware that every dog is unique with their own personality and behavior. However, the steps you will find in these pages will be invaluable no matter what breed your puppy is.

When you bring your dog home for the very first time, knowing where to start can seem daunting. Not only do you have to consider the additional costs of bowls, beds/ crates, food, toys, leashes and so on, but you also have to bear in mind how much training is involved. Knowing where to begin with puppy training can seem arduous, to say the least. But one step at a time.

From the very first day, your patience and level-headedness are essential. It's also very important to note that your puppy is undoubtedly extremely nervous and anxiety-ridden too - so you aren't the only one(s)! Providing your puppy with a stable environment within the first days and weeks after bringing him/her home cannot be overstated.

Dogs are extremely perceptive animals and

they develop impressions about their surroundings very quickly much like their wolf and other canine ancestors.

Enthusiasm and excitement are going to be inevitable for all owners during the first few days. This is great and you should by all means be ecstatic to be bringing home your adorable bundle of joy. At the same time, this excitement can lead to an unhealthy start if you are not careful. It isn't uncommon to find puppy owners and families wanting to play with the puppy, feed him/her, cuddle them and be overbearing in a short and intense period of time. While this emotional attachment might seem like a positive thing, you should try your best as an individual/couple/family to remember that puppies are easily overwhelmed, especially at a young age, and this level of emotional nirvana isn't the best for your puppy.

*So what **do** you do?*

The important thing to note about puppies is that just like other infant canines, they work out hierarchy very quickly. Establishing order is something they are experts at. If you let your puppy sleep on your bed the first night and don't put in place set-in-stone rules, this will work against you very quickly. In fact, studies have time and time again shown that puppies who were trained from the very first day comprehend obedience three times better than puppies who weren't trained until the second month of being in a new household.

What's more is that if you don't establish your rules and are lazy on puppy training, when the novelty of owning a new puppy wears off, your new fluffy friend will end up breaking the rules and you'll be the one struggling to clean up after him/her. By all means be happy and ecstatic but remember that you got a puppy to love and protect. Much like a child, this comes will rules, boundaries and ensuring your puppy doesn't take over and exhibit bad behavior which becomes even more of a problem as he/she gets older.

Another reason why discipline from day one is so crucial is that when puppies are separated from their mother, their psyches are in the utmost vulnerable state that they can be in. This means that they are extremely impressionable and are looking for both a sense of belonging and a community.

This must be used to the puppy's advantage by showing them true care. Such true care means not smothering them with ridiculous levels of physical affection but by being somewhat affectionate while ensuring your puppy develops a progressive understanding of his/her place in the family. Routine is part of this understanding.

Giving Your Puppy Attention

Now that the essential basics have been covered, let's get right down to it. On day one, you'll bring your puppy home. With all of the aforementioned advice in mind, you need to instruct your puppy of the rules in the correct manner.

Rule Number #1:
Don't spend all your time with your puppy

This can be hard because 'oh look how cute he/she is'. Yes, puppies are adorable but their appearance should not be a reason to let them off the hook with bad habits and behavior. When I say do not spend all your time with your puppy, what I mean is carry on with your day as you normally would. If you're going to be out of the house and at work all day while he/she is all alone, then your puppy has to get used to that as soon as possible. The same applies if he/she exhibits vocal cries or moans.

Do not rush to their attention because this teaches him/her to be dependent and shows them that you will be there at every call. Trust me when I say that this method works. Puppies are far more independent and impressionable than human babies and as such, they pick up behavior patterns very quickly.

Another thing to ensure when you first get your dog, is that you are not strict or harsh with your puppy. Never raise your voice at him/her and do not scare or intimidate them.

At such a young age, puppies are not trying to misbehave or do wrong. Their actions are based on natural urges for what feels right in their mind. Shouting at a puppy leads to trauma and a fragmented relationship with them. Do not do it!

On the contrast, demonstrate what behavior you do want to see. The best way to encourage this is to show him/her how to play with toys. Throw/squeeze/roll a toy and when your puppy chases after it, jumps, chews a toy or reacts playfully, stroke and/or cuddle him/her to establish a sense of achievement. This lets your puppy know that he/she did something that made you happy while feeling happy himself/herself. This is positive reinforcement and a healthy way to train your puppy from the first day.

On the first day, you will see acts of deviance from your puppy. Remember: he or she does not know any better yet so when you see him/her doing something bad such as jumping on a bed or chewing a pillow, say 'off!' with a firm but not strict voice and place one of his/her toys nearby to show him/her what they ought to be playing with/jumping on/chewing instead. Again, showing him/her praise and stroking him/her is essential for them to know they are doing the right thing.

A key thing to add to your day one to-do list is to find your local veterinary clinic and book an initial appointment. It is indispensable to ensure that a professional clinician talks you through vaccinations, dentistry and other healthcare which could crop up in the future. A side-note to this is to make sure you do not let your puppy outdoors until the vet gives a thumbs up.

2

Leash Training

Let's talk about the role of the leash and what to do when training your puppy to use it. I mention it early on in this book since it is more important than puppy owners realize. Getting this right from the get-go ensures success as your puppy grows out of puppy-hood and into adulthood.

You might be wondering why there is a chapter dedicated to leash training - after all, isn't it simply a case of putting a leash on your young dog and allowing them time to get used to it?

In principle, yes! But the reality is, it takes

takes many puppies a long time to figure out what a leash is for, so they tend to bite at it and more often, they'll tug and pull on it. Pulling on their leash is surprisingly common for puppies, especially very young ones. They do this because they feel pressure around their necks and it makes them very uncomfortable and scared. It's a foreign object to them and their canine instincts tell them that it's a threat to them as well as a nuisance.

When leash training, there are two important parts of this area of training - getting your dog used to the leash and helping them to walk on a leash. On the following page, I have laid out the best action plan for leash training your little puppy - bearing in mind maximum comfort and effectiveness.

Leash Training Success - Step by Step

- Ensure you buy a leash that also has a body harness. Bodily support reduces risk and helps your puppy keep their balance.

- Ensure leash is always loose and not tightened in any way.

- Be gentle and comforting when placing the mechanism on your puppy. Have treats and toys at hands if he/she gets stressed out.

- Once the harness and leash are on (loosely), stand up. Next, encourage your puppy to walk as normal. Do not move until your puppy is ahead of you. Make sure he/she is comfortable and not being tugged, even slightly. No pressure should be present apart from the extremely brief moment to change direction.

 - When you feel your puppy pull or tug, tug very quickly to prevent it and then release the leash once more. It's important to enforce the idea that your puppy cannot pull at his/her will. This is important from a young age to instil into their minds.

Remember not to reward pulling and only give your puppy a treat when he/she obeys your movement and comes to you when he/she feels that (VERY BRIEF) split second tug. A tip that must be stated here is that you should purchase as soft a harness as you can find and only use harnesses during practice. Never leave it on. When your puppy grows older you can start introducing regular walking collars.

3

House-training & Potty-training

This chapter is all about what is arguably the most important aspect of puppy training - potty-training or as we like to call it in the canine loving world 'housetraining'. House-training at its core is principally about making 100% sure your puppy goes from being wild with his/her toilet habits to being a well-trained young dog who understands the rules of the house and knows how to control their bladder - only using the allocated space for doing his/her business.

In essence, your puppy must be aware of where he/she is allowed in the house and what is off limits. I must make clear that navigating a new environment can be challenging for puppies. They're new to your house and it's a lot bigger and more complicated than it would be for a human counterpart. Not to worry - we have you covered in this chapter!

An initial note is that house-training a puppy can be very stressful and quite frustrating…well…*really* frustrating - but the good news is that all puppies get there eventually and in their own time. What you will notice very quickly with your puppy is that he/she is a little cr*pping machine. When they're young, puppies grow at a pretty rapid rate and thus, they eat more food since they require more energy. What's more is that since they haven't yet learned about controlling their bowel and bladder habits, it can seem like they are voiding themselves constantly.

Needless to say, you need to be patient with your puppy as he/she learns how to develop their 'den' instinct - the instinct which tells them not to go when they are in the 'den' (household). When they are amongst their mother and the rest of the litter, puppies are used to having the freedom to urinate and excrete wherever and whenever they desire.

Principles of Housetraining

As I've stated multiple times already, your patience is invaluable when it comes to caring for and training your puppy.

* Please note that puppies cannot be fully house-trained until they are about 5 or 6 months old. *

The first step of housetraining is simple: you need to supervise your puppy to see how often and where they do their business. After you've worked out their habits, you need to quickly assert the rules. In fact, there are 6 vital rules when it comes to housetraining.

GOLDEN RULES OF HOUSETRAINING

1. Decide where your puppy's toilet area is - usually a soil patch outside in a garden but in proximity to the house. This can be hard if you live in the city in an apartment or do not have access to outdoor spaces. In these instances, use a corner of the bathroom and set up a sort of litter box. Alternatively, an outdoor plant.

2. Allow them frequent (more than adult dogs) access to this area.

3. Use positive reinforcement (such as treats and toys) when your puppy successfully uses the toile area.

4. When you do work out your puppy's pattern, develop a schedule for regular

feeding and using the toilet area. This instills a sense of routine in your young dog (this is undoubtedly the most important rule).

5. For the first two to three weeks, keep a diary of your puppy's toilet habits.

6. Do not punish or scold your puppy when he/she is learning their routine. They will make mistakes so be level-headed.

- -

It is vital that you give your puppy time. As mentioned in the introduction, every puppy is different and some take longer/shorter to learn. A common question dog-owners ask vets and in online forums is why their dogs aren't learning faster. The time-frames in books and pamphlets are always rough guides. Some dogs can take much longer but as long as you love your puppy, your attitude during this process will determine everything.

I often get asked how often an average puppy goes. It isn't abnormal for a puppy to frequent the toilet every 30 to 50 minutes. This varies from food to dog and you also have to take into account the kind of chow you're feeding him/her and if they had treats. Also bear in mind how much/little water your puppy drank You'll be pleased to know that puppies sleep a lot and for a long period of time. They don't tend to need to pee or poop during this time.

While you are keeping a little diary of your puppy's schedule, also take one or two occasions in the night to ensure that your puppy is in his/her pen/crate/bed. Every dog owner can affirm that puppies love to wander about late at night. Keep an eye on them initially and make sure that they aren't getting themselves into unsafe mischief. If he/she is found wandering about or chewing the furniture, pick him/her up gently and with utmost care and place them back in their crate.

A top tip about housetraining is to feed your puppy regularly and at the same times. This speeds up the process because the in/output of food-excrement ratio will become routine pretty fast. Needless to say, always double-check that your puppy has sufficient amount of water in his/her bowl.

How will I know when my puppy needs to go?

I desperately wanted to address this frequently asked question. It's true that in principle, you set up a designated area and your puppy goes to the toilet. But in reality-you just don't know when they need to because a dog will simply poop when he/she needs to often unprecedented. Even worse is when your puppy has their routine but on the way to using the toilet, they go on the floor half-way there.

Not to fret - there is a sure-fire way to handle this all-too-common scenario.

The solution is trial and error but will inevitably work. You have to work out when you fed your puppy. After 30 minutes (preferably just before, around 25 mins), take your puppy to his/her spot. Set them down. Wait for about five minutes and if your puppy doesn't need to go, leave it. Do this for a couple of days until they do go in the right place and make sure you give them as much praise as possible when this happens.

Rewarding a puppy lets them know 'oh I pooped where I was meant to' and they'll begin to associate pooping in that area with reward and pleasure. Believe me, they'll very quickly be more than willing to do their business their if a reward follows.

With time, your puppy will learn that their business must be done in one place. This creates a new dilemma. At night time, they'll start to cry, whine and howl calling you that they need the bathroom. When this happens, swiftly take them to their area and reward them once they're done. Put them straight back to bed.

Obviously, when they're older, they'll take the initiative to do this upon themselves. This process can take two to three months as bladder and bowel control does take time. They are learning so be patient but firm with the rules. Note that if you have a puppy of a larger breed of dog, use a loose leash to lead them to the toilet area.

I will also say that while pooping and needing to go is spontaneous in puppies, some do exhibit little warnings. These are usually circling a small area with their head down, sniffing excessively and low-level whining. Like human infants, you'll get to know your puppy pretty quickly and their behavior/personality etc.

A small but useful piece of advice to make your life easier when you're going to sleep is to bring your puppy to his/her toilet area just before you head to sleep. Sometimes he/she will need to go and other times not. However, giving them a chance to use the toilet before bed can save your sleep from being disturbed later in the night when your fluffy friend whines and howls.

What if I'm out and/or don't have time?

This is a common complaint among first time dog owners who have a busy life. The reality is, most of us have jobs to get to and lead lives that render us unable to be at our puppy's every beck and call. Not to worry, there is such a thing as 'passive dog training' or 'passive puppy training'. Whichever you like to call it, this involves house training them while you aren't around. The primary way to do this is to restrict your puppy to a puppy-proofed area of the house (preferably their toilet area). This gives them the freedom to go when they want and without your presence but it also instills in them the concept of knowing they can only go in a certain part of the house. If you choose this method, place the crate/pen, toys, food, water and everything he/she will need while you're out of the house.

The first couple of times you do this, it isn't uncommon for your puppy to shred up the paper, chew things and just be a little mischievous puppy. Don't get angry at him/her, this is completely normal. Once your puppy demonstrates knowledge of where to go and more stability, you can begin to introduce him/her to another puppy-proofed room of the house.

When people adopt puppies, there is a misconception that it is an easy process. It certainly isn't but it *is* rewarding! Consistency, patience and undying love for your dog are all the keys to successful training. Your puppy is a living and breathing animal so owners ought to expect that they'll be a handful at the start. This shouldn't sway owners from caring for and keeping a puppy because the love they will give you throughout their and your life cannot be underestimated.

Also, your puppy might not always show their appreciation for all you do but animal behaviorists have shown in their research that puppies do see **you** (the owner) in some way as his/her mother/father. They do have love for you but being responsible in these initial stages is so vital for your puppy to grow up to be the perfect companion and a happy and healthy dog.

4

Crate Training

Now that housetraining is out of the way, let's go straight to **crate training**. You might be wondering what in the world crate training is.

Crate Training :

(definition)

Crate training is where you train your puppy or dog to associate their crate/cage as a safe space or safe location.

This is especially important as they begin to develop their 'den' instinct which all dogs possess. Crate training isn't easy - that much ought to be emphasized from the get-go but with persistence it can be a good way to help your puppy navigate their new house before they're ready to roam free.

Crate training can take up to 4 weeks although most puppies can be successfully trained within 2 to 3 weeks. Again, it all depends on the temperament, personality and playfulness of your puppy. What I will say from the start is that crate training is TEMPORARY and should not be a way of imprisoning your dog or restricting them for long periods of time. This borders into cruelty and so it is so key to get it right if you are going to use the crate approach.

Until puppies are fully house-trained, they should not be able to roam about as they please throughout the household. Not only is this a health and safety issue for your pup, but it's also so that they learn that they cannot pee and poop where they please. The last thing you want is to be cleaning your house of mess all the while having a disobedient puppy.

Before we get to how to crate train, I will note that there is an alternative to this method. Some owners prefer confinement training. This was briefly touched upon earlier but to elaborate, confinement training is where you limit a puppy's access to a puppy-proofed room of the house where he/she has everything he/she needs. Utility rooms, well-sized conservatories and kitchen areas are the best.

In both confinement and crate training, you are not keeping the puppy captive and you must ensure that all their needs are met. Positive reinforcement albeit with toys, kisses, cuddles, treats or otherwise is essential in both - regardless of which one you try.

So now that this distinction has been clarified, let us talk about what crate training involves. Confining him/her to a conservatory (for instance) is an effective way to housetrain your puppy and aids them in understanding their limits on where to pee and poop. It moreover signifies to them that they are not permitted to use the rest of the house as a toilet area. The main purpose of crate training is to discourage your puppy from peeing or pooping when in confined spaces so that they will be encouraged to do so when let out. In this process, he/she will learn to find the designated toilet area which you have set out for them. Another benefit of crate training is that it teaches them to control their bladder and bowel.

I cannot state clearly enough that the crate method is temporary and you should not exceed two hours of it. It can have detrimental effects otherwise. Unlike confinement which provides your puppy with everything he/she needs for a long period of time while you're out, crate training should only be performed under your presence and supervision for a short period.

So how do I crate train my puppy, the right way?

It's very simple - let your puppy out every hour and take him/her to their toilet area. Once there, allow them up to ten minutes to use the space for their business. For whatever reason, if he/she doesn't need to go, just repeat the process and during the occasions that he/she does do his/her business, reward them appropriately. If your puppy is especially young, do keep them in the crate for longer than 30-50 minutes.

Just like I said earlier, keep a diary of how your puppy is getting along. This not only helps to keep track of progress but can prove to be an invaluable record if your vet ever asks about your puppy's bowel/bladder habits.

Mistakes can and do occur during crate training, so as always, be patient and consistent when things don't go to plan.

5

Managing Your Puppy's Emotions

Puppies, just like all canines, are emotionally complicated. They have varied needs and sometimes, it's not always obvious what the problem is. In this chapter, we'll explore how you can identify and manage common behavioural issues that your little one might face.

Howling, Barking and Crying

The most common one is when your puppy howls, cries, whines and moans. As a first time dog owner it can be hard to know what your puppy is trying to tell you.

In this chapter, we'll go in depth to help you navigate the common reasons your puppy is so vocal and the psychological implications of the messages they convey in this manner. After this has been established, you'll be taken through the steps on what to do and what not to do.

Puppies whine and cry. This is a fact for 99 if not 100 per cent of young dogs. The most common reason is fear which is why you might notice that your puppy cries most when he/she is isolated and alone. Remember that when puppies are taken from their mothers, they can be traumatized. This is why it's important to reassure them and make sure they know that they're safe. Much like wolves, puppies will whine and howl when alone. In the wild, canines do this when abandoned. It's therefore normal but more often than not, puppy owners who aren't used to this worry that something is horribly wrong. This is especially the case in breeds that produce very loud cries. Not to worry though, we'll guide you through what you need to know.

The harsh reality is that you need to train your young dog that isolation and being alone in general are natural parts of life and so, in the first instance, unless it's late at night and your dog needs the toilet, you should not answer and rush in every time they cry. This applies when you're around the house and you hear her/him cry. Do not instinctively give them attention because they need the tough love of being on their own sometimes. In nature, it would be the same thing. If a young dog cries out, not every cry will be answered. This is important so that your puppy can develop a healthy relationship to you, other people and other dogs (this will be covered later on).

A significant reason why you shouldn't give your puppy attention every time he/she cries is because they will begin to learn that you will always be there and this can create a sense of control over you in his/her mind. This isn't good because otherwise you could very feasibly have a badly behaved puppy on your hands.

Other than fear and loneliness, puppies whine and howl when they aren't used to their environment/crate/house/pen yet. In instances where you've given your puppy space and he/she still whines after a week or 10 days, then do spend a little more time with him/her than you usually would. If after you've tried this for three days and he/she still whines, it's time to be a little bit stern. When you leave and he/she carries on crying, assert firm but not harsh dominance with a shout. Usually this is the word 'no!' said abruptly but some owners shout 'hey!' or 'shush!'. If he/she quietens after a few minutes, praise your puppy and cuddle him/her. They need positive reassurance when they have behaved well. You certainly don't want your puppy thinking you don't love them or that they aren't wanted.

They will also begin associating your departures with privacy and will quickly become accustomed to the idea of being alone sometimes. The good thing is that they know you'll return which provides comfort in their minds.

Many puppy owners believe that the second their puppy begins crying, they have to act. This is wrong. Always give him/her the benefit of the doubt and allow them to cry/whine for a short time. When you hear your puppy being vocal, just wait a few moments. If he/she persists, assume that he/she needs the toilet. If this turns out not to be the case, bear in mind the steps on the previous two pages.

Also keep in mind that your puppy might just be reacting to an environmental change. It isn't uncommon for a puppy to cry if he/she is cold, hungry or even thirsty. If you have other pets, your puppy might be afraid of them at first. Use rationale first before assuming anything about your puppy. They are complex, just like we are.

With regards to puppies who are attention-seeking which is common also, remember not to necessarily give in to them and never praise them when they've been badly behaved. It's always best to give them space and a non-harsh but firm command. At the same time, you shouldn't let your puppy feel too lonely. Abandonment can be hard so they need some affection from you - more as they become house trained fully!

I still can't work out why my puppy is crying!

I've heard this one a million times and truthfully speaking, yes, puppies do whine for no reason sometimes and it can be difficult to know what to do when you've tried everything to settle them and comfort them.

Canines love to vocalize - it's what they do and especially at a young and vulnerable age, their whines can be uncontrolled and constant. While they seemingly whine for no reason, it's only 'no reason' from a human perspective. Usually, they have a reason but it's very challenging to work it out when it isn't hunger, loneliness, thirst, feeling uncomfortable or needing the toilet.

In such instances, rule out as many possibilities as possible. If you have and you're still confused, the reality could be that your puppy has learned a bad habit. In most cases of dogs that I've worked with, excessive crying, howling or whining is the result of bad training. These puppies have learned that they can get what they want by whining. This results from owners who gave them way too much attention, owners who gave them too many treats, owners who let their puppies get away with everything, owners who did not give their puppies space or any sort of vocal reprimand and so on.

It's hard to get your puppy to unlearn this but instant action is needed. The best solution for young puppies is just to start re-training them into good housetraining habits. If your puppy is getting older and more mature, retraining can be very arduous, to say the least. In this case, you'll need to change their routine a bit. A great way to get them to stop whinging all the time is to let them get more exercise every day, and putting them on socialization programs with other dogs can work wonders! While keeping your puppy more busy than usual, start to distance yourself a little bit from them since it's likely they are used to being the center of attention. Again, use the firm 'no!' to teach them about independence. A balance of care and isolation is what you must aim for. Not abandonment nor over-affection!

When you succeed with handling your puppy's whining habits, it's important to keep an eye on them. If for whatever reason, after a month or so, your dog exhibits unusual crying, a health problem could be to blame. It's therefore essential to get them to their vet as soon as possible!

Biting

My puppy likes to bite. What do I do?

Aside from whining, crying and howling, puppies, especially while their teeth are coming through, love to bite. It's very normal and most dogs grow out of it because their mother teaches them against it at a young age.

If your puppy is especially young, you'll need to train them not to bite before the 5 month mark. Before giving you the instructions of how to stop your puppy from biting, it's crucial to learn why puppies (and dogs who are new to a house/family) bite in the first place.

I previously said that puppies whine when lonely and isolated. Some puppies can feel intense loneliness and this develops into what dog-experts call 'fearful aggression'. These puppies use biting as a way to try and scare people/other dogs off when they are afraid.

Aside from fear, lack of socializing with other humans and dogs causes them to bite too. Since they were taken away from their sisters and brothers of their mother's litter, it's up to you to ensure they get adequate time with their own species and are socialized with people the correct way too. More on this later.

Another reason why a puppy will bite is if they dislike you, perceive you as a threat or do not respect you as an authority figure. Just like any dog owner will confirm, trust and respect are essential for your relationship with your dog. You must take it upon yourself to respect your puppy and in turn they will respect you. This applies to discipline as well. As aforementioned, positive reinforcement, rewards and affection are essential for your puppy's respect for you. If you are too stern like many bad owners are, your dog will not respect you and will resent you forever. Scolding never works so do not do it! Whenever you are training your puppy, make sure your love for them is visible. With vocal reprimands when you tell them off, it must be followed by a reward when they do the right thing.

Socialization

It's time to talk about socializing your puppy correctly. Dogs are social creatures - this means that they have hierarchies within their packs. Just like humans, social animals need to interact with others for optimal mental health. Isolation leads to horrible consequences like biting, uncontrolled barking and aggression.

Puppyhood is therefore the best time to start your little friend on their social adventures. It is believed that the best duration for social training is 3-4 months although socialization has to be an ongoing process thereafter. You may begin this process from the day you get your puppy.

How to Successfully Socialize Your Puppy

1. Encourage friends and family members to meet your puppy. Your puppy needs to become acquainted to new people, smells and personalities.

2. Safely bring your puppy to social events, the mall, shopping, school events if you have children and so on.

3. Take your puppy on car rides.

4. Once house-trained, let your puppy explore items of clothing, bags, boxes and so on where new experiences, smells and textures can become a part of their sensory experience.

5. Encourage friends who have pets to meet your puppy, even if they aren't dogs!

6. Don't hesitate to vacuum around your puppy: he/she needs to become used to sounds of the human world.

7. Let your puppy explore leashes, collars and so on so that they become used to different objects.

- -

With all of these tips, I will state that you should expect your puppy to be frightened and uncomfortable at times. This is normal and if they are especially afraid, wait a few days and try the activity again.

A lot of puppy owners think they can tell their dog's emotions from how they look. This is a myth and an anthropomorphization of dog behavior. It's best to monitor their habits and physical behavior.

6

Obedience Training

This chapter will cover obedience training which can be challenging if you aren't too sure where to begin. For the sake of simplicity, this chapter will be broken down into the various aspects of obedience and discipline.

- Obedience and Discipline
- Name Recognition
- Coping With Excitement

Successful Obedience and Discipline

We will first address obedience and discipline which will feed nicely into the next two parts of this chapter. Obedience training is a core element of puppy training but it does not necessarily prevent all emotional issues in young dogs. What obedience training is particularly useful for is enabling a central sense of communication between your puppy and you.

While it sounds relatively harsh, obedience training is simply the term used to describe when you want to teach your dog to do something. This can be anything from sitting to fetching and even staying still and calm in stressful situations. We spoke about social structures in canincs in the chapter 'Day Four' but obedience training helps to develop a sense of social structure in the household between your dog and his/her owner(s) i.e. you.

The rewarding aspect of obedience training is that when your puppy listens and obeys you, it means that he/she is demonstrating clear love and respect for you. Compliance is what you want out of the exercise. However, it isn't a question of rendering your dog scared - not at all - in fact this would be counterintuitive. Instead, obedience training draws a line between you, the dog's carer, and your puppy who is subordinate in the structure of the household. Teaching your puppy or young dog tricks such as raising their paws when you raise your hand playfully can work wonders and dogs actually like learning this form of communication. It is a healthy way to show submission to you.

All in all, obedience training should be light-hearted and an effective way of bonding with your puppy. A common thing that people say is that you can't train a puppy! This is a misconception and in my experience with dogs, puppies can and do learn effective means of communication during this sort of training. To say that a puppy cannot learn obedience is to say that they have no personality and awareness. This is completely wrong since they have a lot of both. I believe as do many, that the earlier you start training a dog, the better. Their behavior isn't always going to be predictable so the younger you start training them, the better the chances are for long term success.

For obedience training, I would highly

suggest that you research training centres and classes in your local area. Trained professionals can work wonders for your puppy and it's also a beneficial social experience for them. You don't need to send your puppy to more than a couple of classes but it is suggested by many vets and carers that puppies do attend one or two classes for the basics. The rest can be done by you at home.

So, how do I start?

You start obedience training wherever you want. It's best if it's outdoors and in the so-called 'real world' because while there are distractions, your dog needs to get used to them as quickly as possible. Obedience training is really down to you. Whether that's gently lifting their paw and saying a catch-word which identifies it over and over until they associate the sound and movement with the action or whether it's teaching them to sit and stay, it's up to you.

A common obedience training method is car obedience whereby you help your dog to practice staying calm and seated in your car. Remember not to actually drive during training. Let your dog become accustomed to the space, smell, and environment of the vehicle. After a few minutes of initial sniffing, exploration and intrigue, your puppy will settle down and that's when you can take them inside and do the same thing five or six times before practicing driving with them in the car. Start with small, safe and local trips and if your puppy starts to whine or get excited, vocal reprimanding can be enforced aiding in car obedience training.

You're probably sick of hearing this but reward is the important part of obedience training. Do not fail in showing your puppy contentment and praise when he/she stays, sits, fetches or other actions. They deserve it and they will know how to act in accordance to your rules from then on.

Calling and Name Recognition

Name recognition is a frequently discussed subject in the world of puppy ownership. Owners have trouble choosing a name and also in enforcing the name when getting the puppy to recognize those instances when he/she has been addressed directly.

To most puppies, hearing their name or being called helps to register in their minds as 'time to run' and so they scurry away from you. This is because they identify commands with being pushed to do something or with discipline and/or danger or threat. This must be reversed and is a more advanced part of training.

Here, we will talk about getting your puppy to recognize not only when they are being called but to actually approach and respond to their name. Before telling you all about what you should do, it's key that we cover what not to do (the things that a lot of owners don't realize they are doing wrong).

One of the most terrible things you can do as an owner when training your young puppy to come to you at the command of their name, is to allow them off their leash - especially in public. Many owners erroneously believe that it's completely fine to let their dogs run free without their leash and do other things that do not involve the owner. In doing this, you are telling your puppy that 'fun' and 'exercise' are things that do not involve you. As such, they will not associate you with that pleasurable sentiment and freedom. Moreover, when it comes time to go home, you put the dog back on the leash and suddenly, YOU'RE the bad guy because in their minds, you've ended the good time they were enjoying. This can be troublesome for your relationship with your young dog and can lead to unwanted tension and disrespectful behavior on their part.

What you're also informing your puppy is that it's much more worthwhile to disobey than to end the fun. So what can you do as an owner to get your dog to come when called and respond to their name?

Quite simply, you need to instil within his/her mind that being called is not a bad thing. They need to associate you and your demand of their presence as something positive for them. Dogs are intuitive, as I've stated a few time already and something unique to puppies is that they are constantly trying to work out when we are instructing them and when we are being passive with them. The ideal situation in calling your dog is if they identify pleasure with your presence when you want them and they acknowledge that they're being instructed. Another scenario you do not want is upon successfully teaching your puppy to come to you but they think it is a punishment. A lot of owners do manage to get their dogs to come to them but only to clip their nails, give them a bath or something else unpleasant for the dog's wishes. You will need to do these things of course, but in the first few weeks and months, when calling your dog and getting his/her attention, it's best to play with them, give them treats, cuddles, toys, kisses and so on. Nothing demanding or taxing for them.

Let them want to come when called because of this association with pleasure and fun. Eventually, they'll understand that being called is an act of love from you to them.

I will once more put onus on how great behavior and obedience classes can be for young dogs and it will save you a lot of stress in the long run. After one or two sessions, you should aim for 10 to 15 minutes a day of calling training. It does get easier with time though. It's pushing through these initial stages and laying down a good foundation that requires some effort.

I now want to take you through practical

steps for perfect 'Coming When Called' training.

- -

Coming When Called

1. Preparation

Just like any element of young dog and puppy training, preparation is everything. Step one is to ensure your puppy actually wants to learn and isn't tired.

At meal time, take a treat or piece of food and place it near your puppy's nose. If he/she does not respond, try waving it gently. If he/she is still not interested, come back later and try another time. When your puppy is ready and does show interest to the food, it's time for training.

2. Secrets to Getting a Puppy's Attention

Now that you're ready and your puppy is too, feed your puppy a limited amount of food from your hand - not more than two or three pieces of chow or kibble. Inevitably, your dog will want more if he/she is hungry.

Step back a little bit with food in your hand and watch as your puppy is intrigued and wants the food. Say 'here girl/here boy! Come here!' or something of the same iteration. Stretch your food hand out towards his/her nose and your dog should approach. If he/she does, reward her with praise and cuddles. Give them the food right away. This ensures they know they'll be rewarded in this 'little so-called game'.

Next, lower yourself to your puppy's level while simultaneously holding their collar gently. They'll get the message and when they approach closer, give them more food.

It is recommended that you repeat this exercise every day until it becomes natural. The same principles of this exercise can be applied to calling your dog over to play but instead of food, the reward is a ball/toy/treat/cuddles.

When your puppy gets the hang of the food calling training, you'll need to progressively decrease the food rewards but keep the same 'come to me' principle in mind. For the best training, rewards should not be given every time. Only when he/she comes especially quickly and in a direct manner. This means your dog doesn't take advantage of your kindness or the situation on the whole.

Coping With Excitement

It's time to talk about something that every puppy owner can attest to - excitement. While excitement can be cute and a sign of a positive and happy-go-lucky puppy, too much of it can become a hinderance in training and can become a burden pretty fast! Why? Because when excited, some puppies urinate uncontrollably and chew excessively as well.

If your puppy training experience is going well but you're still finding the odd puddle of urine here and there or your puppy still likes to chew when happy, it's time for a specialized action plan.

Firstly, we must appreciate that puppies who do pee when excited often have bladder control issues and in these puppies, it's just a question of you needing to housetrain your puppy for a bit longer than expected until it stops. Your puppy doesn't necessarily know he/she is doing anything wrong so do not reprimand harshly.

If his/her bladder is under control and you're still having issues with an over-excited puppy who urinates around the house, you may simply need to ensure that he/she doesn't get himself/herself in an over-excited state to begin with. The best sure-fire way to do this is to make sure they are getting sufficient playtime, social time and outdoor time. Let them go crazy during these times so that they won't feel the need to be over-excited when inside the house.

Many owners complain that their dog urinates when they return home or someone new arrives at the house. In these cases, it's always best to ignore your puppy. Ignore them up to five times until they get bored and realize that you aren't interested in their over-excitement. Remember : DOGS LOVE ROUTINE and this helps them a great deal with understanding boundaries - and it helps you in not having to clean up as much pee.

Play is very important - especially with the owner present.

Barking and Howling

Earlier, we delved into coping with a puppy who whines and cries. As time goes on though, dogs vocalize through barking.

You don't say!

As a puppy or young dog owner, I'm sorry to tell you this but you'd better start getting used to the fact that your puppy will bark. It's just what they do. I've met dog owners who complain about barking but many fail to bear in mind that telling a dog not to bark is like telling a human not to talk. However, barking and howling does become a problem when it's excessive. Dogs know that they can communicate emotions vocally - and they do use their vocal capacities to do so. In this segment, we'll look at why excessive barking occurs and how to control it. That way, you won't have those annoying neighbors knocking on your door at all hours in the night.

The first kind of problem barking occurs in dogs who feel like they need to 'let out' or release energy which is pent-up. A lot of these dogs do feel confined and somewhat lonely. So, the first thing to assume if you have a barking dog is to add extra outdoors and play time to the schedule. Allow them to exercise more and release tension which has undoubtedly built up for a while.

In fact, you'll want to do this as soon as possible because many dogs begin to enjoy barking and use it as a substitute to physical exertion. This is a huge problem so make sure it doesn't get to this stage by letting your dog out (on a leash) more than once a day or until their barking reduces to a normal amount.

Alternatively, your dog might bark as much as they do because you accidentally conditioned them that way. You might be wondering what I'm talking about. As a young puppy, some owners respond to every one of their dog's whines and howls with a treat or with a response. Your dog might have ingrained in their brain that they can control you this way and talk to you using the mechanism which seems to have worked until now.

How do I get my dog to bark less?

What you must do in the first instance is cure the underlying cause of barking. As aforementioned, this is most likely to be a lack of exercise or intense emotion (boredom, fear and so on). Obedience training is another solid solution as there are many professionals trained in this area. If you opt out of this, I would suggest you spend more time with your dog because it could just be a case of lack of attention. Too much and too little attention are detrimental to your dog's overall mental well-being.

In cases where your dog does get sufficient exercise and outdoors time, perhaps he/she is in desperate need of socialization - albeit with other dogs or people. Dogs get lonely and some do bark in excess when isolated from others. A quick solution is to spend time with him/her and also to go on a walk with him/her on a leash. Roaming the neighborhood after work hours or on a Sunday can provide your dog with great little social adventures of meeting new people. Dogs love to be the center of attention and they know when people find them cute. Help them to boost their ego and let them revel in the moment.

Just as important as outdoor time and socializing is feeling a sense of belonging. If you work long hours and your dog is home alone for a lot of the day, he/she might not feel a part of the family unit. Play games with him/her more often, give her more love, cuddle with her/him while on the couch and just integrate your dog into more everyday parts of your family life.

*Can I teach my dog to **stop** barking?*

To an extent, yes!

Believe it or not, unless told to do so, dogs aren't aware that their barking causes you or anyone else a problem. If they did, it would be much simpler to get them to stop barking or to reduce how much they bark. Therefore, you need to learn how to train your dog that barking is not a good thing and that it is in fact a nuisance.

Establish this rule for your dog :

It's okay for you to bark until you are told to stop!

Just like every other obedience command, telling your dog to stop barking is a command of instruction. Do not get it confused with a reprimand such as 'no!' or 'off!'

The way it works is as follows. Every time you hear your dog barking, allow two barks. If he/she continues, use the command 'stop barking boy/girl!' When doing this, have a treat at hand that she/he can smell/see. The magic here is that your dog will undoubtedly stop barking because they'll be far too fascinated by what you have for them. They'll sniff the treat and likely eat it.

Now what will happen is he/she will be distracted for a while but nine times out of ten, he/she will bark again soon. When he/she does, bring another treat in front of him/her but do not let him/her have it right away. Wait ten seconds until he/she is completely quiet and willing to take it. She/he will eventually catch on to the fact that staying quiet = yummy treats and this tends to work rather quickly.

Be patient. It might require three to five times of trying before your dog understands what is being asked of him/her. The idea is to get him/her to understand that not barking means that he/she gets rewarded. After a short while, they'll willingly do this without much prompting. Do keep in mind that dogs do use barking as a mechanism of communication so even if after a while of your dog being trained he/she barks abnormally, suspect that there is a health problem and take him/her to the vet. Especially in younger dogs but older ones too. It's never a good idea to push back vet visits - don't take the risk.

Separation and Isolation Anxiety

A common behavioral pattern exhibited by puppies is separation/isolation anxiety. Unfortunately, people are quick to blame the owners for puppies who cannot detach emotionally from them - this is a misconception. Puppies do not like to be alone, this is a fact. Some experience higher than normal levels of sadness and anxiety when you do leave them alone though. They demonstrate these emotions clearly and in destructive ways - crying, biting, chewing things and urination.

When your puppy is showing signs of isolation and not wanting to be left alone, it is vital that you occupy them with new things. In their minds, the world is limited to you, food and treats. Expose them to more toys and allow them to play with/be interested by new obstacles through play. Balls, stuffed cubes and noisy toys tend to work best - in my experience of owning and looking after puppies. Another great way of keeping them occupied is to introduce them to other puppies at designated play areas (on the Meetup app, these exist in big cities and some towns). Alternatively, if feasible, get another pet to keep them occupied but this is just a suggestion.

In addition to adding more toys to their little life, plan time that is just dedicated to playing with them. It helps if there is more than one of you (a partner, friend, relative, child etc). Puppies like to be stimulated and it helps their excitement and overall happiness.

Puppies that Jump

A final area of puppy training that I want to address is jumping - something that is common in almost all puppies. Puppies are social - very social actually - especially when you compare them to the young of other mammalian pets. As such, they love to show us affection and a well-known way young dogs do this is by jumping on us. How many times have you been in a park or taking a walk and a happy dog has sniffed, licked or jumped up at you? Chances are, quite a few!

Puppies do get particularly excited and it's a big deal for them when they get the opportunity to exhibit their anticipation and happiness for someone with affection.

Jumping is a mechanism they use to expel that energy is a vivid manner. It's a form of greeting in all dogs. Just to clear something up - puppies, when very young, will usually waddle to you and lick but as they get older, jumping does become a habit.

While jumping is usually fine and needs no training or discouragement, there are times when jumping becomes immoderate and happens too often. Excessive jumping can be dangerous if there are young children or senior citizens around.

When dogs jump, they also pounce and have a quick wit about the execution of the landing. This can be a problem and somewhat burdensome.

So why do some dogs jump and pounce all the time?

You might find this hard to believe but actually, it is us, the owner(s) who is to blame! The way we raise puppies is the problem, to be more specific. Let me explain. When a puppy is young, we bend down to lower ourselves to them. As they start to grow and learn to be more effective jumpers, we give in and find is more simple to just let them come up to our level with the famous jump-greet.

Who can blame us though - we walk upright on two legs. But even if we can't help it, we condition dogs to come up to our level instead of taking it upon ourselves to consistently lower ourselves to theirs.

What makes this habit worse is how enthusiastic *we* are when we allow our dogs to jump on us. This tells the dog that it's completely acceptable for him/her to do this. Not only are we passively accepting it, but in the minds of our beloved fluffy friend, we are endorsing it wholeheartedly.

Therefore, think how confusing it must be for a puppy or young dog when you OUT OF THE BLUE tell them that it's not okay to do the thing you essentially trained them to do when greeting you. Most of the time, they'll ignore your sudden disapproval and continue doing it.

Solving the problem of a jumpy dog or puppy does not constitute of unlearning the habit, but rather, teaching them a new and better means of greeting you and other humans.

The most effective way is to teach him/her to stay and to sit/stay put when they do jump up. It'll take time but be persistent. The first step is to start lowering yourself to them for cuddles and kisses. Get yourself and your dog into this habit. Encourage visitors to your house to do the same thing and don't take no for an answer. If your puppy or dog doesn't listen to you and continues to jump on the person, pull your dog off of them and firmly assert a reprimand like 'no!' or 'off, now!'

Consistency is important as with all training that has been covered but with this particular kind of training, it is re-training. This means it's harder for your dog to learn and to be consistent in. You are undoing a natural habit which they were previously accustomed to. It's crucial to stick at it every day until you see improvements.

Conclusion

I really do hope that you found this guide to be useful. It is designed to provide an overview which should be a tool for raising your puppy. Training a puppy isn't a one time event - it lasts until they are fully grown and even beyond. A dog is a companion and there is a trust factor which needs to work both ways.

If you respect and love them, they're the most rewarding animals to own, whether you rescued them or bought them. Dogs can be one of the best elements of the human experience and ensuring they grow up happy and healthy begins with you looking after them and training them properly during the earliest stages of puppyhood.

Puppy training isn't always straight forward and mistakes will be made. Every animal is an individual and not all sizes fit all when it comes to advice but the principles of this guide are a good outline to get you started.

I wish you the best of luck with your puppy!

\- \-

Printed in Great
Britain
by Amazon